we love you...
One Direction

A 2014 ANNUAL

Written by Becky Bowden
Designed by Duncan Cook

Contents

The Rise to Fame

One Direction shot to fame after their sudden and unexpected success during the X Factor 2010 auditions sent them hurtling to worldwide stardom. Entering the TV show and competing as five individual acts originally, it wasn't until a certain ex 'Pussycat Doll' Nicole Scherzinger suggested that they should

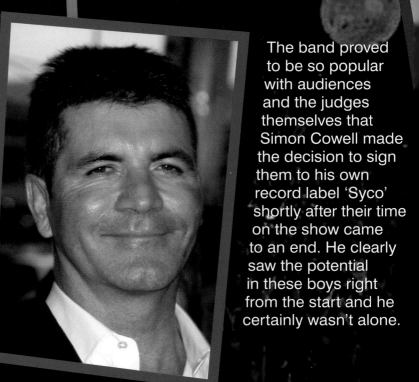

combine and create one big super group, that their career as we know it really started to take shape. Good call, Nicole!

The band consists of five members: Niall Horan, Zayn Malik, Liam Payne, Harry Styles, and Louis Tomlinson. They finished in third place on the X Factor's seventh series.

The band proved to be so popular with audiences and the judges themselves that Simon Cowell made the decision to sign them to his own record label 'Syco' shortly after their time on the show came to an end. He clearly saw the potential in these boys right from the start and he certainly wasn't alone.

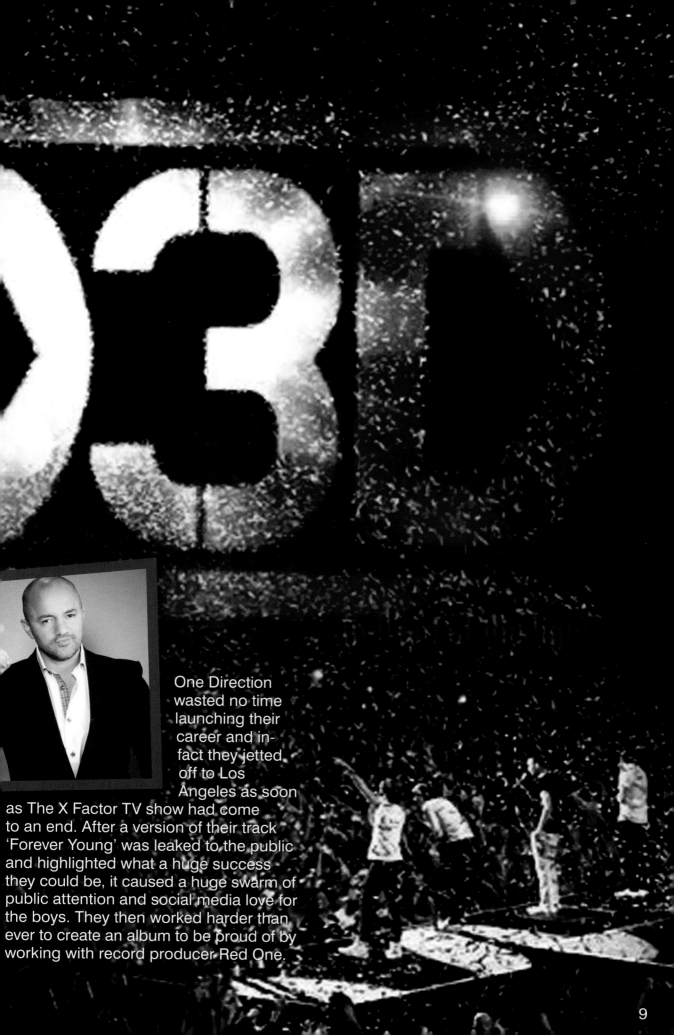

One Direction wasted no time launching their career and in-fact they jetted off to Los Angeles as soon as The X Factor TV show had come to an end. After a version of their track 'Forever Young' was leaked to the public and highlighted what a huge success they could be, it caused a huge swarm of public attention and social media love for the boys. They then worked harder than ever to create an album to be proud of by working with record producer Red One.

The boys seemed to gel almost instantaneously as a solid group, surprising everyone in the record industry at the strong bond they had formed in such a short time, considering they'd never even met before taking part in The X Factor. Everyone wanted to know more about this hot new band on the pop scene and they soon found themselves signing book deals, taking part in interviews and making the front pages of all the top magazines.

In September 2012 they released their debut single "What makes you Beautiful" which reached number one in the singles chart and left fans practically screaming for more! The boys were understandably elated and this track was soon followed up by a string of successful hits including "Gotta Be You" and "One Thing" which were equally well received and earned them one of the strongest fan-bases any boy band has ever seen.

After successfully managing to work their magic on fans in the US and impressing record label bosses across the pond, One Direction's first album "Up All Night" was released globally in early 2012. It actually became the UK's fastest-selling debut album of 2011!

The boys went on to release a string of singles and albums that have all been

hugely popular all around the world. They have had an overwhelming effect in the public with their infectious pop sound and show absolutely no sign of slowing down any time soon. After a string of number one hits, their single "Live While We're Young", released in September 2012 had reached the top ten in almost every country it charted and was also recorded as the highest one-week opening sales figure for a song by a non-US artist in the US. Impressive stuff, boys!

One Direction are hot property in the music scene and their sell-out tours reflect this. Their first tour was popular enough, but their second concert tour in February 2013 (the Take Me Home Tour) spanned over 100 shows in Europe, North America and Australasia. Ticket sales reached 300,000 within a day of release in the UK and Ireland, which included a six-date sell-out at London's The O2 Arena, proving that fans were keen to see their idols live in the flesh and on the stage and were willing to go all out in order to do so!

With a 3D movie biopic of One Direction also being released in 2013, these boys are determined to prove that there really is only One Direction and that leads straight to the top! What's next boys – world domination?!

Spotlight on **Harry Styles**

NAME:
Harry Edward Styles

D.O.B:
1st February 1994

FAMILY:
Mum, Dad, Step-dad and
1 older sister

LIKES:
Tattoos, food and fast cars!

DISLIKES:
Harry has a big fear of snakes

FAVOURITE FOOD:
Tacos and sweetcorn

FAVOURITE FILM/S:
Chick-flicks like The Notebook,
Love actually and Titanic!

FIRST CONCERT:
Nickelback

SPECIAL SKILL:
Juggling

FACT:
He made a very brief cameo in Ed Sheeran's
first video for 'Drunk', this was filmed
backstage at London's Shepherd's Bush Empire

Spotlight

on Liam Payne

NAME:
Liam James Payne

D.O.B:
29 August 1993

FAMILY:
Mum, Dad and 2 older sisters

LIKES:
Keeping himself fit and healthy, girls with nice eyes, genuine people

DISLIKES:
Cheats and fake people

FAVOURITE FOOD:
Bacon, steak and healthy vegetables

FAVOURITE FILM/S:
The Toy Story Trilogy

FIRST CONCERT:
Gareth Gates

SPECIAL SKILL:
Beatboxing

FACT:
After becoming ill when he was a baby, Liam suffered years of tests until he was aged four when doctors discovered that one of his kidneys was scarred and dysfunctional. He then had to have up to 32 injections a day to cope with the pain. He's so much better now though but likes to take care of his body and keep fit

Spotlight on **Louis Tomlinson**

NAME:
Louis William Tomlinson

D.O.B:
24 December 1991

FAMILY:
Mum, Dad, Step-dad and five half-sisters

LIKES:
Football, Driving his fast cars and surfing

DISLIKES:
People who chew their food too loudly, hearing rumours about himself and the band that aren't true

FAVOURITE FOOD:
He's not fussy and will eat anything! He is partial to a big bowl of Special K cereal though. Louis also loves Yorkshire tea and always makes sure that the band has plenty in supply when they go on tour

FAVOURITE FILM/S:
Everything from action to comedies!

FIRST CONCERT:
Busted

SPECIAL SKILL:
Talking to animals

FACT:
He's not just a pop star! When he was just 11 years old, Louis was lucky enough to grab a spot as an extra on the ITV drama Fat Friends. Dragging the family along for the fun meant that his new born sisters Daisy and Phoebe also starred as babies on the show. He also went on to have parts in TV shows such as 'If I had you' and 'Waterloo Road'

Spotlight
on Zayn Malik

NAME:
Zayn Javadd Malik

D.O.B:
12 January 1993

FAMILY:
Mum, Dad and 3 sisters

LIKES:
Intelligent Girls, The band NSYNC and all of the 1D fans who he says are like part of his family… aww!

DISLIKES:
Liars, Swimming and Open Water

FAVOURITE FOOD:
Pasta with Bolognese or spicy chicken

FAVOURITE FILM/S:
Scarface

FIRST CONCERT:
JLS

SPECIAL SKILL:
Drawing

FACT:
Zayn's favourite song of all time is 'Thriller' by Michael Jackson

Spotlight on Niall Horan

NAME:
Niall James Horan

D.O.B:
13 September 1993

FAMILY:
Mum, Dad and older brother

LIKES:
Football and girls with nice smiles

DISLIKES:
Going without food for too long and being in small or confined spaces

FAVOURITE FOOD:
Sausage and mash, pies, creamy chicken pasta, chicken kiev

FAVOURITE FILM/S:
Grease, Goodfellas and The Godfather

FIRST CONCERT:
Busted

SPECIAL SKILL:
Playing guitar

FUN FACT:
Before the band were named One Direction, Niall apparently suggested they should be called 'Niall And The Potatoes'

SPOT THE DIFFERENCE

These two pictures may look the same but there are 10 differences.
Can you spot them?

PICK THE HABIT

We all have our own little bad habits that we sometimes wish we could shake and the boys are no different. Can you guess which habit belongs to who?

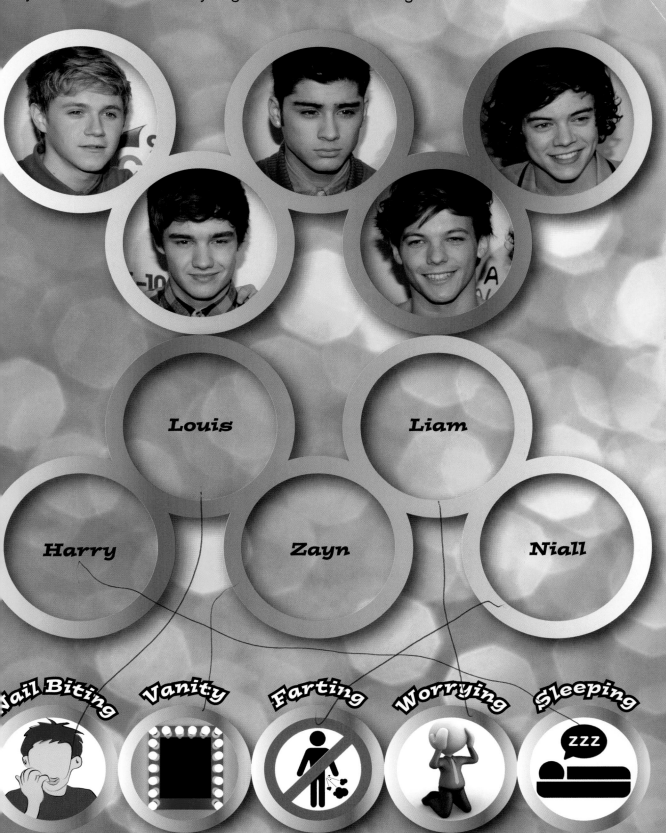

Louis

Liam

Harry

Zayn

Niall

Nail Biting

Vanity

Farting

Worrying

Sleeping

ANSWERS ON PAGE 60.

What We Love

We all know that WE love One Direction, but what things do the boys love? Here are a few of 1D's all-time favourite things!

Movies

The One Direction lads are all massive movie fans. So much so that they're regularly spotted out and about at some of the most star-studded premieres and hanging out backstage at various celeb launches.

It has even been rumoured that Liam Payne has splashed out on an Iron Man replica for his home, due to his love of the movies and their star, Robert Downey Jr.

Maybe Liam is taking inspiration from his band mate Zayn, who also has a movie replica in his house. It just so happens to be a life sized Storm Trooper from Star Wars and is apparently located in his hallway. Imagine bumping into that in the dark!

source - sugarscape.com

Food!

One Direction are growing guys, of course they are going to be huge fans of food! Whether it's takeaways, healthy foods or sweet treats, the 1D lads are always snapped munching away.

Liam is the band mate who always tries to eat healthily, mainly because of the problems he suffered with his health when he was a lot younger. His kidneys may be in good condition again now but this 1D member is taking no chances and is definitely the most health conscious of the bunch when it comes to food and his body in general.

Niall, Zayn , Harry and Louis all seem to enjoy a bit of comfort food, home cooking and of course Nando's or pizza! Who can blame them when they're on the road as much as they are?

Charity

All of the band have kind, caring and charitable natures. Maybe that's why they have managed to bond so well together as a group in such a short period of time?

They are regularly asked to take part in events, signings and giveaways for charities and often give up a large chunk of their time, dedicating it to spending time visiting hospitals or participating in events and charity galas to help others less fortunate than themselves.

Touring!

1D love being on tour and getting to share their music with the fans at their various live venues! We can only imagine what mischief these five lads find themselves in.

Speaking to GQ Magazine about whether they find themselves attracting a lot of female attention on tour, Liam answered: "Honestly, because we're taken from the venue to the hotel and whatever else you don't really see much in between. We don't really go out, but this tour will be different – because we're all 18 now…"

The guys also have their own onesies that they wear on the tour bus to keep them warm and toasty in the colder weather. How cute!

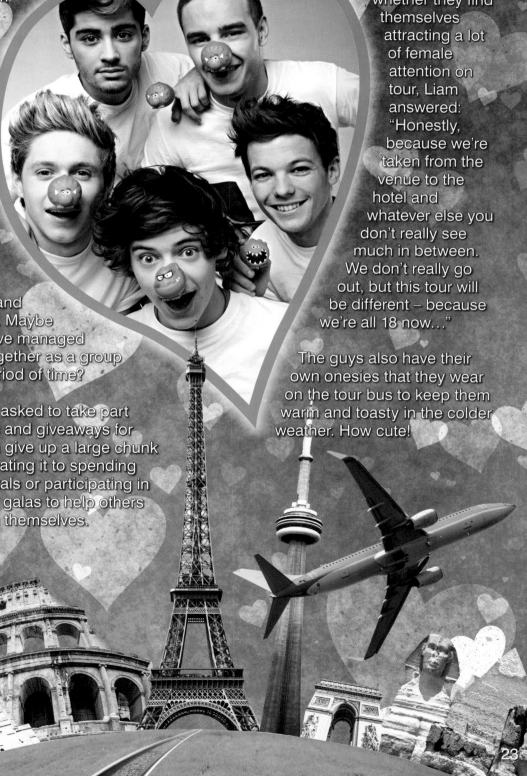

Live on Stage

Performing their final U.S. show at Bank Atlantic Center, Florida.

The boys perform at the Patriot Center in Fairfax, Virginia USA.

One Direction performing in Verona, Italy.

One Direction perform live in the Rockefeller Center , New York.

Live at the Sanremo Festival, Italy.

Performing on TV at Musique Plus in Montreal, Canada.

Performing at Hordern Pavilion, Sydney.

Closing Ceremony performance at the London Olympics

Kicking off their blockbuster
'Take Me Home Tour' with a matinee
performance at London's O2 Arena.

Performing at The Arena at
Gwinnett Center in Atlanta, Georgia
on June 26, 2012.

Live at BankAtlantic Center
in Sunrise, Florida.

Rocking the house
in Washington, D.C. June 2013.

On stage during the Bambi award
ceremony in Duesseldorf, Germany.

Live at the Plymouth Pavilions, Devon.

ONE DIRECTION

Live show at Planet Hollywood,
Las Vegas.

Performing in Durham,
North Carolina USA.

Quick-fire Lyrics Quiz

We all enjoy singing along to our favourite One Direction songs, but how well do you really know all of the lyrics? Test yourself with our quick-fire lyrics quiz below. If you get stuck, don't panic! The answers can all be found at the back.

1

WHAT MAKES YOU BEAUTIFUL

You're insecure,
Don't know what for,
You're turning heads when you walk through the door,
Don't need make-up,
To cover up,
...../.../.../..../.../... is enough.

2

LIVE WHILE WE'RE YOUNG

Yeah, we'll be doing what we do,
Just pretending that we're cool,
And we know it too (know it too),
Yeah, we'll keep doing what we do,
..../........../..../..../.... so tonight.

3

LITTLE THINGS

You can't go to bed,
Without ./..../../... ,
And maybe that's the reason
that you talk, in your sleep,
And all those conversations
are the secrets that I keep,
Though it makes no sense to me.

4

CHANGE MY MIND

Lean in, when you laugh,
../..../........... ,
There's no music on,
But we dance along,
Never felt like this before,
Are we friends or are we more,
As I'm walking towards the door,
I'm not sure.

5

SAME MISTAKES

Yeah, yeah, that's what, crazy is,
When it's broken you say
....../......../../.... ,

And you pray, pray, pray,
That everything will be okay,
While you're making all the same
mistakes.

Answers on page 60.

1D
Star Signs

CAPRICORN

Zayn's birthday is on 12 January 1993, making him a Capricorn. Louis is also a fellow Capricorn, with his birthday being 24 December 1991.

Element: Earth
Birthstone: Garnet
Ruling Planet: Saturn
Symbol: The Goat
Capricorn character traits: Powerful, motivated and forward thinking. Capricorns like to be in control of their lives and work hard to get where they want to be. This seems pretty relevant to both Zayn and Louis! Capricorns also often like plenty of attention and enjoy long-term relationships.

AQUARIUS

Harry's birthday is on 1 February 1994, making him an Aquarius.

Element: Air
Birthstone: Amethyst
Ruling Planet: Uranus
Symbol: The Water Bearer
Aquarius character traits: Aquarians are deep thinkers who always have other people's best interests at heart. They are kind, caring and have unique personalities that make them stand out from the crowd. Like Harry, Aquarians are also usually very outgoing, sociable people.

VIRGO

Liam's birthday is on 29 August 1993, making him a Virgo. Band mate Niall is also a Virgo, with his birthday being 13 September 1993.

Element: Earth
Birthstone: Sapphire
Ruling Planet: Mercury
Symbol: The Virgin
Virgo character traits: Virgos are typically known to be strong willed and creative. That sounds like Liam and Niall! They make great friends and companions and can be deep and thoughtful people at times with a playful nature when they let their guard down.

Awards & Recognition

YEAR	BY	NOMINATED FOR	WON/NOM
2011	In: Demand Honours	Best Fans	Winners
2011	In: Demand Honours	Best Group	Winners
2011	In: Demand Honours	Best Guest	Winners
2011	In: Demand Honours	Best Newcomers	Nominated
2011	In: Demand Honours	Best Song "What Makes You Beautiful"	Winners
2011	In: Demand Honours	Best Video	Winners
2011	The Sun: Bizarre Readers Awards	Best Pop	Winners
2011	Virgin Media Music Awards	Best Group	Nominated
2011	Virgin Media Music Awards	Best Video "What Makes You Beautiful"	Nominated
2011	4Music Video Awards	Best Breakthrough	Winners
2011	4Music Video Awards	Best Group	Winners
2011	4Music Video Awards	Best Video "What Makes You Beautiful"	Winners
2012	ARIA Awards	Best International Artist	Winners
2012	Bambi Awards	Pop International	Winners
2012	BBC Radio 1 Teen Awards	Best British Album "Up All Night"	Winners
2012	BBC Radio 1 Teen Awards	Best British Music Act	Winners
2012	BBC Radio 1 Teen Awards	Best British Single "One Thing"	Winners
2012	BRIT Awards	British Single "What Makes You Beautiful"	Winners

YEAR	BY	NOMINATED FOR	WON/NOM
2012	Guiness World Records	"Up All Night" went straight to no.1 in the US Billboard Charts, making 1D the only British band to have ever achieved the feat with their debut album.	Record
2012	JIM Awards	Best Newcomer International	Winners
2012	Los Premios 40 Principales	Best International Artist	Winners
2012	Los Premios 40 Principales	Best New International Artist	Winners
2012	MTV Awards	MTV Artist Of The Year	Winners
2012	MTV Europe Awards	Best European Act	Nominated
2012	MTV Europe Awards	Best New Act	Winners
2012	MTV Europe Awards	Best Uk & Ireland Act	Winners
2012	MTV Europe Awards	Biggest Fans	Winners
2012	MTV VMA's	Best New Artist	Winners
2012	MTV VMA's	Best Pop Video "What Makes You Beautiful"	Winners
2012	MTV VMA's	Most Share Worthy Video	Winners
2012	MTV VMA's Brazil	International Artist	Winners
2012	Nickelodeon Kids' Choice Argentina	Artist or Group International	Nominated
2012	Nickelodeon Kids' Choice Argentina	Favourite Song "What Makes You Beautiful"	Winners
2012	Nickelodeon Kids' Choice Brazil	Favourite International Artist	Winners
2012	Nickelodeon Kids' Choice Mexico	Favourite Song "What Makes You Beautiful"	Winners
2012	Nickelodeon Kids' Choice Mexico	International Artist	Winners
2012	Nickelodeon Kids' Choice	UK Favourite UK Band	Winners
2012	Nickelodeon Kids' Choice	UK Favourite UK Newcomer	Winners
2012	Teen Choice Awards	Breakout Group	Winners
2012	Teen Choice Awards	Love Song "What Makes You Beautiful"	Winners
2012	Telehit Awards	Most Popular Artist	Winners
2012	Telehit Awards	Best International Pop Group	Winners
2012	Telehit Awards	Song Of The Public	Winners

Year	By	Nominated For	Won/Nom
2012	The Sun: Bizarre Readers Awards	Best Pop	Winners
2012	UK Music Video Awards	People's Choice "Live While We're Young"	Winners
2012	4Music Video Awards	Best Group	Winners
2013	Billboard Music Awards	Billboard 200 Album "Take Me Home"	Nominated
2013	Billboard Music Awards	Billboard 200 Album "Up All Night"	Nominated
2013	Billboard Music Awards	Top Artist	Nominated
2013	Billboard Music Awards	Top Billboard 200 Artist	Nominated
2013	Billboard Music Awards	Top Duo/Group	Winners
2013	Billboard Music Awards	Top New Artist	Winners
2013	Billboard Music Awards	Top Pop Album "Take Me Home"	Nominated
2013	Billboard Music Awards	Top Pop Album "Up All Night"	Nominated
2013	Billboard Music Awards	Top Pop Artist	Winners
2013	Billboard Music Awards	Top Social Artist	Nominated
2013	BRIT Awards	British Group	Nominated
2013	BRIT Awards	BRIT's Global Success	Winners
2013	JIM Awards	Best Group	Winners
2013	JIM Awards	Best Pop	Winners
2013	JIM Awards	Hottie of the year Harry Styles	Nominated
2013	JUNO Awards	International Album "Up All Night"	Nominated
2013	Los Premios 40 Principales	Best New Artist	Winners
2013	MTV VMA Italy	Best Band	TBC
2013	MTV VMA Italy	Best Fan	TBC
2013	MTV VMA Japan	Album of the year "Take Me Home"	TBC
2013	MTV VMA Japan	Best Group Video "What Makes You Beautiful"	TBC
2013	MTV VMA Japan	Best New Artist	TBC
2013	Much Music Awards	International Video of the year – " Kiss You "	TBC

YEAR	BY	NOMINATED FOR	WON/NOM
2013	Much Music Awards	UR Fave International Artist/Group	TBC
2013	Nickelodeon Kids' Choice Awards	Favourite Music Group	Winners
2013	Nickelodeon Kids' Choice Awards	Favourite Song	Winners
2013	Nickelodeon Kids' Choice Awards Australia	Aussies Fave Hottie – Harry Styles	Nominated
2013	Nickelodeon Kids' Choice Awards Australia	Aussies Fave Music Act	Winners
2013	Nickelodeon Kids' Choice Awards Australia	Aussies Fave Song One Thing	Winners
2013	Nickelodeon Kids' Choice Awards UK	Favourite UK Band	Winners
2013	NRJ Music Awards	International Duo/Group	Winners
2013	People's Choice Awards	Favourite Album " Up All Night "	Winners
2013	People's Choice Awards	Favourite Breakout Artist	Nominated
2013	People's Choice Awards	Favourite Music Fan Following	Nominated
2013	People's Choice Awards	Favourite Song "What Makes You Beautiful"	Winners
2013	Radio Disney Music Awards	Best Music Group	Winners
2013	Radio Disney Music Awards	Fiercest Fans	Winners
2013	Radio Disney Music Awards	Song Of The Year	Nominated
2013	Virgin Media Music Awards	Best Group	Nominated
2013	World Music Awards	World's Best Album "Take me Home"	TBC
2013	World Music Awards	World's Best Album " Up All Night "	TBC
2013	World Music Awards	World's Best Group	TBC
2013	World Music Awards	World's Best Live Act	TBC
2013	World Music Awards	World's Best Song "Little Things"	TBC
2013	World Music Awards	World's Best Song "What Makes You Beautiful"	TBC
2013	World Music Awards	World's Best Song "One Way Or Another"	TBC
2013	World Music Awards	World's Best Video "Live While We're Young"	TBC
2013	World Music Awards	World's Best Video "What Makes You Beautiful"	TBC

What a Year!

So, what have One Direction done during the course of the past year? Why have they made headlines and how busy have their mega-popstar lives been? Get the lowdown here.

This Is Us

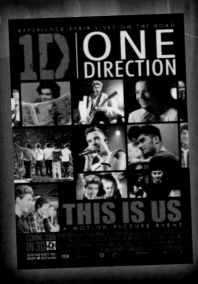

One Direction released their very first movie and of course, these lads don't do anything by halves so it had to be in 3D didn't it! The movie made its premiere on August 29th in the UK and launched all the way around the world at roughly the same time.

'This is us' shows us more of what the boys are like in 'real life' when they're hanging out together and when they are on tour or performing. A great way to give fans a glimpse into their world.

One Moment Fragrance

In 2013 One Direction launched their debut fragrance 'One Moment' to excited fans. The fragrance is a fruity, playful scent that reflects the essence of 1D. It captures splashes of fresh fruit and seasonal flowers mixed with undertones of warm musk and should leave an enticing scent on the skin.

The bottle is pink, multi-faceted and has a silver crown on top. Perfect for the millions of female One Direction fans out there!

Harry the Best Man

Harry was best-man at his mum Anne Cox's wedding to Robin Twist. Harry got suited up ready for the big day. He looked gorgeous of course and even wrote the speech himself which lasted around 10 minutes and took all of the guests through a rollercoaster of emotions from roars of laughter to floods of tears.

Harry and Taylor

Who can forget the hugely high-profile but short lived romance that blossomed between Taylor Swift and Harry Styles?

It may not have lasted long but it certainly turned a few heads and was widely reported on in the entertainment industry before the couple made the decision to end their relationship. Were you for it or against it 1D fans?

Charity

One Direction announced that they would be donating a large chunk of their money from the 2014 tour to Stand Up To Cancer charity.

When asked about their reasons behind this charity and the decision to give back, Liam said: "We're so proud to be supporting Stand Up To Cancer while touring the UK and Ireland.

"Cancer affects nearly everyone at some point in their lives so we all need to do what we can to bring forward the day when all cancers are cured. Stand Up To Cancer is all about bringing people together as a collective force and we hope our fans will get involved."

Waxwork Fame

In 2013 One Direction had the honour of becoming waxwork figures at the tourist hotspot Madame Tussauds in London. Apparently the boys look great and are totally realistic so getting your picture snapped with them could be the next best thing for those who dream of meeting these five young heart-throbs!

Word Search

How many of the One Direction related words can you find in the wordsearch below?

```
W B F N R H Y T N C K O R T R G T N Z L H
R G N K W Q W B P P N F M P Y N H R N N M
L C F R P V R C G E C D W O Y X I M V V R
L T L L Z Y J M T K Z N W C G Z S N Z D N
X F J R T T J H W E P N Q Y L X I M Y F M
G N Y M C X I K V F M Y V S Q B S R R J Z
U P A L L N I G H T K O L D Z B U M U L T
N G V R G T H M L N Z N H W B X S V T J L
L U F I T U A E B U O Y S E K A M T A H W
Q H H L I A M G D I W G Z J M R V Y H L Z
T T Q A D Z P M T N N H L V C E N T M R K
L R C T R M C C X I F T E M Y R K H M L G
L L W M T R E W H M P N F R P G M A O T O
R H A L J R Y T L K M E R F E M R U T X T
H B L I I T E L K N R M W M P W I Z K D T
P G P D N L E N R Y L O C J K S E N H Q A
C C E M T W L X T A T M N F Z P R A R M B
R N L T O Y W Q T Z P R Z G W W C W R N E
O R I C R O T C A F X U Q T P N L H D E Y
L L J X Z X V L R J M O X R W H D K Y V O
Y R V N J B W D T A Y L O R S W I F T V U
```

Cowell ✓	Syco ✓
Gotta be you	Take Me Home
Harry ✓	Taylor Swift
Liam ✓	This Is Us
Little Things	Up All Night
Louis	What Makes You Beautiful
Niall	Where We Are
One Direction	X Factor
One Thing	Zayn
Our Moment	

ANSWERS ON PAGE 61.

Whose Shoes?

The name of the game gives it away. Can you match which shoes belong to which 1D member? Go on then, best foot forward!

Story of Success

Many bands have tried and failed to be the next big thing in the world of pop. So what makes One Direction so special?

The band One Direction was quite literally created before the public's very eyes, meaning that from the beginning, we all became part of their story. This now hugely successful band started as five individual singers, each talented in their own way, and came together to create a group who have earned themselves one of the largest fan-bases in pop.

The public have eagerly followed their story every step of the way, from the release of DVDs, movies and books, all charting their success and rise to fame we've felt like part of it all.

Each of the boys have a strong and charismatic personality which has helped them win the stamp of approval from not only teenage fans, but fans

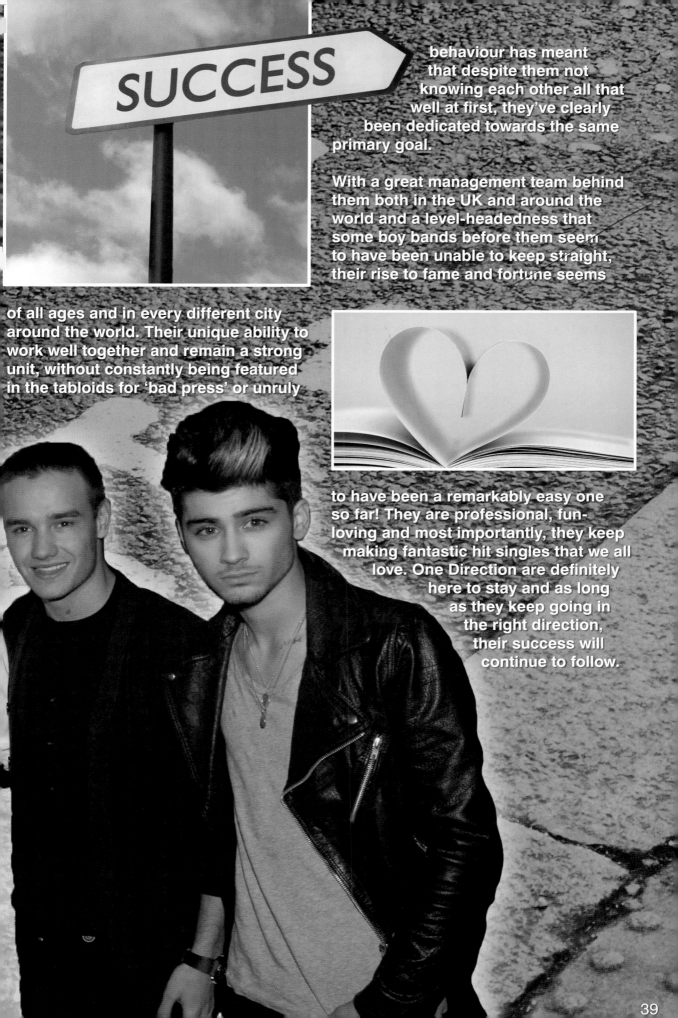

SUCCESS

behaviour has meant that despite them not knowing each other all that well at first, they've clearly been dedicated towards the same primary goal.

With a great management team behind them both in the UK and around the world and a level-headedness that some boy bands before them seem to have been unable to keep straight, their rise to fame and fortune seems

of all ages and in every different city around the world. Their unique ability to work well together and remain a strong unit, without constantly being featured in the tabloids for 'bad press' or unruly

to have been a remarkably easy one so far! They are professional, fun-loving and most importantly, they keep making fantastic hit singles that we all love. One Direction are definitely here to stay and as long as they keep going in the right direction, their success will continue to follow.

Fashion Focus!

A look at what the boys wear, and t[he]ir individual style.

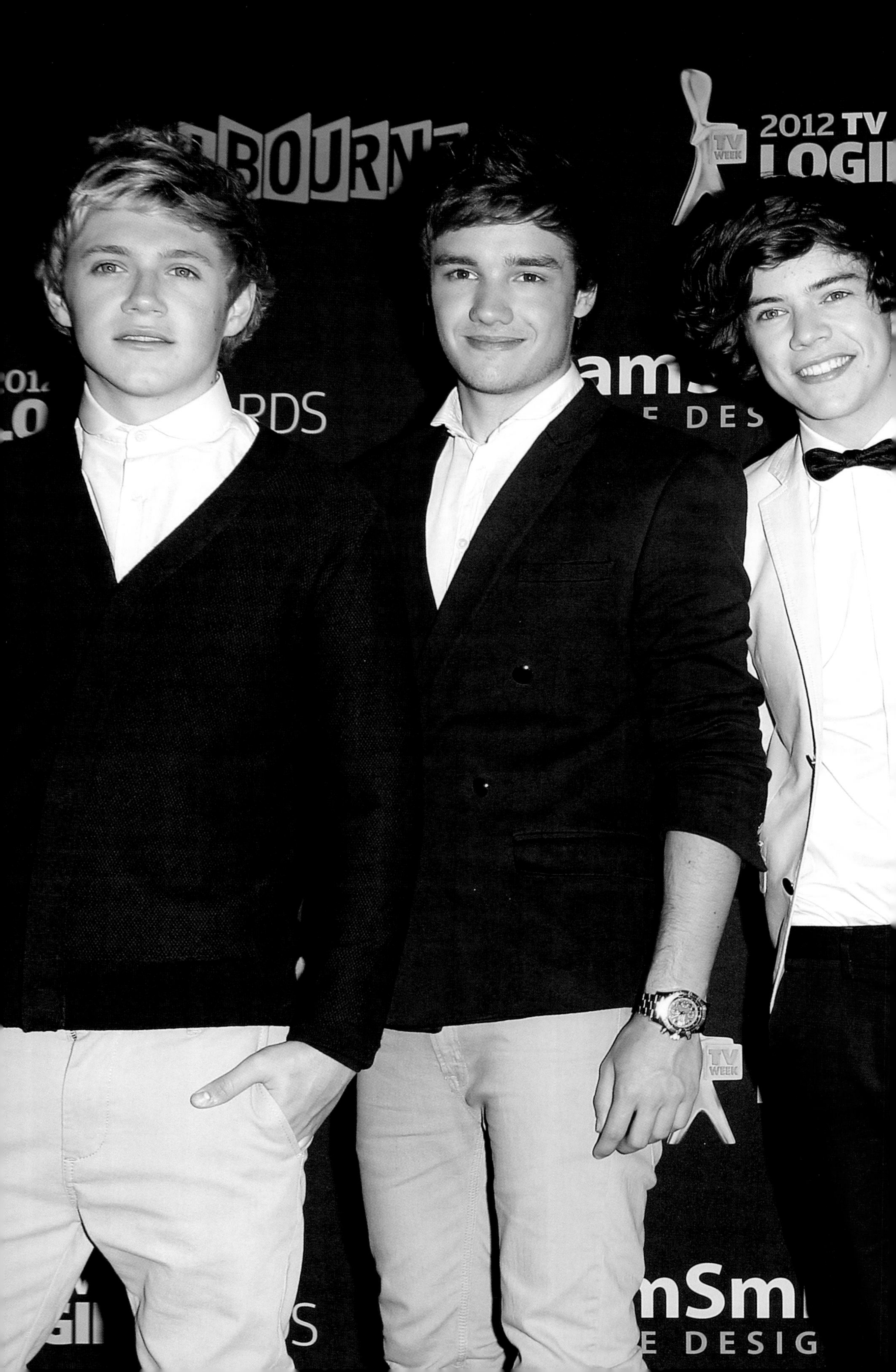
2012 TV
TV WEEK

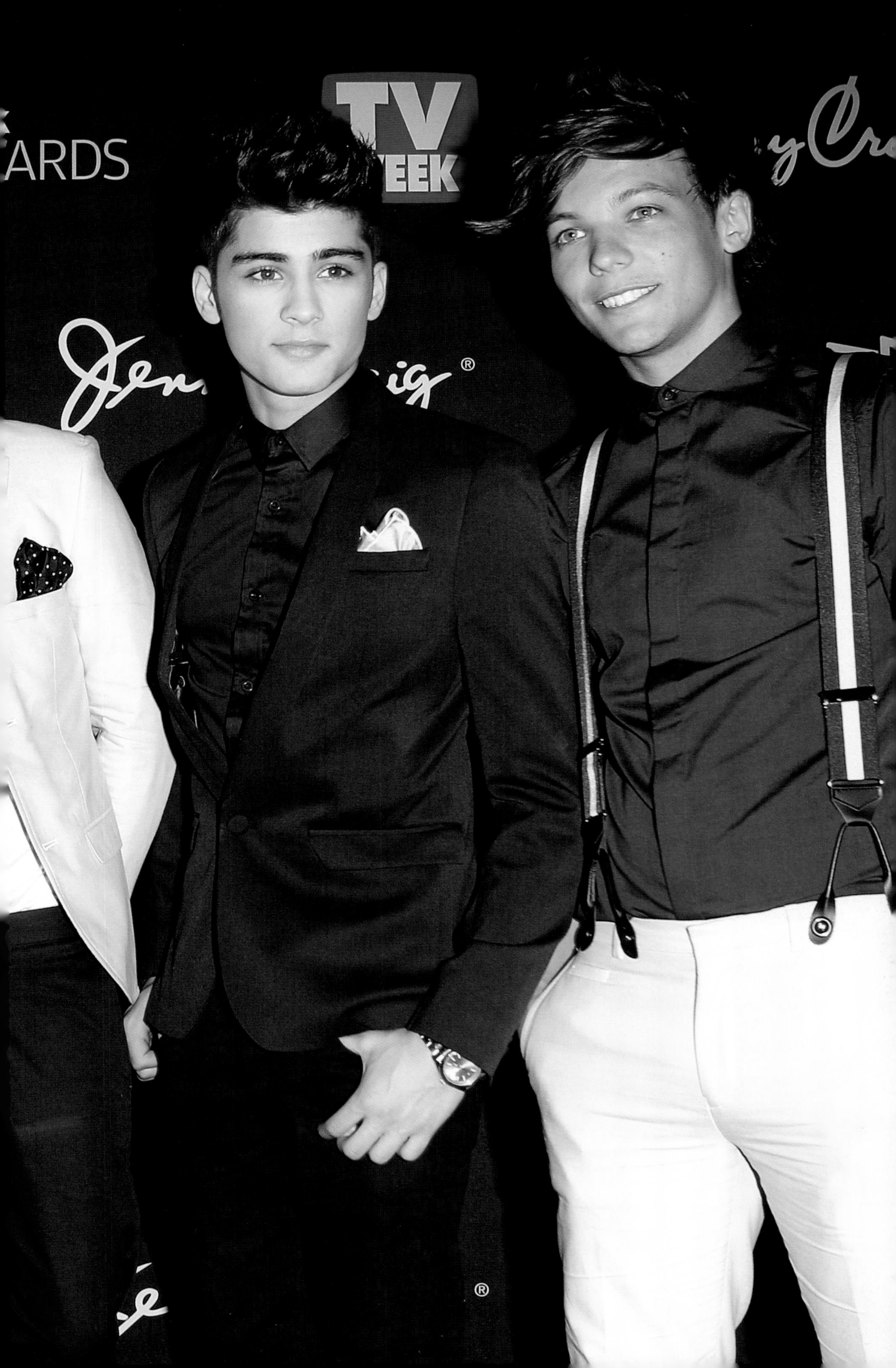
ARDS
TV

Quiz - Know Your Stuff?

So you think you're an ultimate One Direction super fan? Try your hand at our 1D quiz and see how many questions you can get right.

Q 1.

Which TV show made One Direction famous?

Q 2.

What is the name of One Direction's Debut Fragrance?

Q 3.

Name the song that Liam sang at his X Factor audition in 2010?

Q 4.

Which football team does Niall support?

Q 5.

What is the name of One Direction's 3D Movie?

Q 6.

What is the name of One Direction's 2014 Stadium Tour?

Q 7.

Which member of Little Mix has Zayn dated?

Q 8.

Where did Harry work before he auditioned for the X Factor?

Q 9.

Who bought their old Sunday League Football Team?

Q 10.

Complete the title of One Direction's 2013 book: "Where We Are: Our Band, Our ….."

Q 11.

When is Harry Styles' Birthday?

Q 12.

After a long history of illness, Liam has only got one what?

Q 13.

What was Louis's X Factor Audition song?

Q 14.

What was the name of Harry's old band?

Q 15.

What was 1D's debut single?

Q 16.

Liam and Niall both share the same middle name. What is it?

Q 17.

Who suggested that the boys should be put together to form one group?

Q 18.

Which song did Harry sing for his X Factor audition?

Q 19.

What was the name of 1D's first album?

Q 20.

Which member of One Direction had small roles in Fat Friends, If I Had You and Waterloo Road?

ANSWERS ON PAGE 60.

One Direction
Famous Friends

Katy claims she has all of the **1D** dolls and even snatched a kiss with Niall at the 2012 MTV VMAs.

Kate Perry

Cher and the boys starred in the 2010 series of the **X Factor** and have remained close ever since.

Cher Lloyd

Zayn is dating **Little Mix** star Perrie Edwards, and both groups are from the **X Factor** stable so have a lot in common.

Little Mix

Olly Murs

Olly has a great friendship with the boys after the **X Factor** and still has a round of golf with them. Olly also supported them on their US tour last year.

Simon Cowell

Simon just loves the boys and has had them back on the **X Factor** numerous times since they became runners up in the 2010 final.

Robbie Williams

Robbie has never shied away from heaping praise on the lads and thinks they will be bigger than the spice girls.

Nick Grimshaw

Nick is always professing his love for Harry on his BBC Radio 1 show, and has a fond spot for the rest of the band.

Justin Bieber

When **1D** and **Bieber** find time out from their crazy schedules they get together and hang out, play guitar and cook.

James Corden

James is a big fan of the group and made a bee line for their table at last month's Brits, no doubt to catch up on all the gossip.

Ed Sheeran

Ed has penned a few tracks for the boys and has been rumoured to be dating Harry's ex "Taylor Swift".

Louise Thomson

Louise from 'Made in Chelsea' – Louise and Niall reportedly shared a cosy night in together and Louise apparently gushed to friends that he was playing the guitar and singing! What a lucky lady!

One Direction Quotes

Those One Direction lads are a chatty bunch, here are a few of their best quotes and tweets…

All Talk!

TWEETS:

Harry Styles @Harry_Styles 18 Apr
Just noticed #1000daysof1d!
This is amazing, thank you all so much for all your support.. That's a lot of days. We love you .xx

Louis Tomlinson @Louis_Tomlinson 18 Apr
1000 days of being in the band ? Wow that really is incredible :) Amazing that you guys have shaped our career! Thank you so much x

One Direction @onedirection 31 Mar
Off to the cinema this weekend? IMAGINE when you'll be there to watch @1DThisIsUs. We're getting a bit excited. 1DHQ x

Niall Horan @NiallOfficial 16 Jun
Just watched a cut of "This is us" !
Made me look at life so differently!
man I love you guys ! You've changed our lives !

Niall Horan @NiallOfficial 4 Jun
Came in last night! Jumped on my bed and broke it!
So had to sleep on the couch! not the best nights sleep I've ever had ! #NoInnuendos

Harry Styles @Harry_Styles 9 Jun
Jet lag took over, I fell asleep on the floor in my clothes. A meter from the bed. So close.

Harry Styles @Harry_Styles 6 Jun
The 1D fragrance is called (drumroll)…
Our Moment! And it smells like a summers day..

Harry Styles @Harry_Styles 5 Jun
I went to the shop.
I bought lemon curd.
I ate my first lemon curd sandwich for about 12 years.
It was ace.

zaynmalik1D
@zaynmalik 6 Jun
Can't believe we released
a PERFUME today all because
of a tweet we got from you lot ! :)
big love

zaynmalik1D @zaynmalik 2 Feb
Hi everyone, just a quick message to say I love all you guys, without your support I don't know what I'd do :) x

zaynmalik1D @zaynmalik 1 Jan
We wouldn't be where we are now without you all!
So Happy 2013! Love you all! :) x

Liam Payne @Real_Liam_Payne 19 May
Guysssss still can't believe we will be playing stadiums next year!! Thank you all sooooooo much for the constant support and love

Liam Payne @Real_Liam_Payne 21 Apr
Absolute nutter of a taxi driver ATM feels like I'm on a bank job

Louis Tomlinson @Louis_Tomlinson 24 Apr
Sad to hear about JLS . Wish them all the best of luck in what they go on to do.

Louis Tomlinson @Louis_Tomlinson 20 Apr
Can't believe the UK is over , thank to everyone who can to see it. It was amazing :) gonna put my feet up now and watch match of the day!

QUOTES:

The 1D boys talk to Daybreak about their trip to Japan and Ghana for Comic Relief.

When talking about the trip, Harry notes:
"We all kind of went

out there not really knowing what to expect and then we all came back all kind of looking at each other and just kind of going, 'that was the best thing we've ever done. It was amazing."

Zayn went on to add: "In everyday life, you have, like, little problems that we think are so major and then you go over there and you actually see people that actually are dealing with real problems and happen to carry on every day."

One Direction were interviewed in Switzerland and noted the changes in their personalities and confidence since becoming famous.

One of the things I have learned about being in this position is that when I used to go to parties and someone came up to talk to you and you didn't really know them, I wouldn't be able to hold a conversation."

He added: "I would have been a bit shy but I'm not really that shy anymore. Me and Zayn were actually really quiet when we came into the band but now you can't shut us up."

In an exclusive interview with Fabulous Magazine, Harry was asked if he had been sensible with his money. He is quoted as saying:

"My dad, Joe, is a financial advisor and he basically said that for every £10 you make, spend £6 or £7 of it wisely and have fun with the rest. So yeah, I've obviously had fun,

but I'm not being stupid. I've made sure I've done the right things first. I think it's important to buy property, which is what I've done."

That certainly sounds sensible to us!

Naill talks to MetroLyrics.Com in 2012 about the 1D fans:

"I think our fans are a bit like us — they're very fun, like to have a laugh, like to party. I think that's what comes across on our album as well. It's very fun. It's music that you could play at a party, but it also deals with teenage relationships."

He also continued dishing out the praise but turned his attention to fellow musician Ed Sheeran when asked about their friendship, saying:

"Yeah, we're quite good friends with Ed. We always hang out with him. If you listen to Ed's album, you'll know that he is one of the best lyricists I've ever heard in my life. He knows how to string words together like you wouldn't imagine. We were very lucky to work with him. He wrote a song with us for our album called "Moments." He's very up and coming. He's gonna be big himself."

Talking to The Daily Record about the process of recording their album 'Take Me Home' Harry reveals:

"We ate loads of fast food while recording. I think we were in one studio for about two weeks and it was just a rotation of a certain Thai restaurant and Portuguese chicken restaurant over and over again.

"It's very easy to get stuck in there – you end up with studio tan where you just go green because you've been inside for a week."

A-Z

OF

One Direction

A – **ACCIDENTS** - 1D are very accident prone, they nearly burnt down the X Factor house whilst trying to cook pizza, and they flooded the house by leaving the shower on.

B – **BEATLES** – Harry loves the Beatles.

C – **CALENDAR** – One Direction's 2012 Calendar was the UK's bestselling calendar.

D – **DONCASTER** – Louis is from Doncaster, South Yorkshire which is where Jeremy Clarkson comes from.

E – **ED SHEERAN** – Penned a track (Moments) for their 'Up All Night' album, he is also considered a friend by the boys.

F - **FOREVER YOUNG** – The boys' first single if they had won The **X Factor**, which was leaked onto the internet.

G – **GOTTA BE YOU** was the boys' second single, which reached no. 3 in the UK Charts.

H – **HOLMES CHAPEL** – The town in Cheshire where Harry grew up.

I – **INTELLIGENT** – Zayn loves intelligent women.

J – **JLS** along with some other former **X Factor** finalists joined One Direction for the single "Wishing on a Star".

K – **KAZOO** – One of Harry's many skills is being able to play the Kazoo.

L – **LUCKY** – Niall has a pair of white socks that he believes are a good luck mascot.

M – **MINUTES** – 1D's 2011/12 tour sold out in just 12 minutes.

N – **NICOLE SCHERZINGER** – The guest judge on The **X Factor** who suggested the boys get together and form a group.

O – **OLYMPICS** – The boys performed "What Makes You Beautiful" for the closing ceremony of the 2012 Olympic Games.

P – **POKÉMON** – One Direction has featured in adverts for Nintendo's popular game.

Q – **QUEEN ELIZABETH II** – 1D performed "Little things" in front of the queen at the 2012 Royal Variety performance.

R – **RADIO** – 1D fans flocked to Liam's parents' house in search of tour tickets that were being given away by a local radio station when they misunderstood the clues that were given out.

S – **SYCO RECORDS** – One Direction's record label.

T – **TOUR** – One Direction's first UK tour was called "Up All Night".

U – **UNCHARTED SHORES**, is the new name of a US band who was trying to sue One Direction for stealing their name, luckily the boys won.

V – **VIVA LA VIDA** by Coldplay is Niall's favourite song.

W – **WILLIAM** – Louis's middle name.

X – **X FACTOR** – One Direction finished 3rd behind Matt Cardle and Rebecca Ferguson.

Y – **YOUTUBE** – "What Makes You Beautiful" has over 394 million views on YouTube.

Z – **ZAYN** – need we say more?!

The 1D Effect!

So what is it about the One Direction boys that none of us seem to be able to get enough of? We take a look at some of their most redeeming qualities that make them so irresistible!

Niall's Humour

Niall has a cheeky personality that always seems to be a hit with the ladies. He's good looking, he can play the guitar and is never short of a funny joke, phrase or random quote to break an awkward silence! Plus he has an amazing cheeky grin.

Zayn's Eyes

Zayn has gorgeous dark eyes, a mane of dark hair and a great body. He is confident and determined and is always up for a laugh!

Harry's Hair

Harry's hair has become part of his trademark look. Fans love his luscious locks and he's got a great body too. His tattoos have become quite the talking point in the media and show his desire to be unique and independent. He's also generous, down to earth and has a fun personality!

Liam's responsible nature

Liam is definitely the responsible member of the band! He is always giving advice and looks out for his fellow 1D band mates wherever possible. His natural good looks and great physique also help make him completely irresistible of course!

Louis' Loyalty

He's been quoted as saying he's always happier in long term relationships than just a quick fling, making him a great catch. He's caring, loyal and always looks out for those important to him.

Discography

Albums

Year	Name	UK Chart Position
2011	Up All Night	2
2012	Take Me Home	1

Singles

Year	Name	UK Chart Postition
2010	Heroes (as part of X Factor Finalists)	1
2011	Wishing on a Star (as part of X Factor Finalists)	1
2011	What Makes You Beautiful	1
2011	Gotta Be You	3
2012	One Thing	9
2012	More Than This	86
2012	Live While We`re Young	3
2012	Little Things	1
2013	Kiss You	9
2013	One Way Or Another (Teenage Kicks)	1
2013	Best Song Ever	2

ONE DIRECTION
ONE THING

ONE DIRECTION
LIVE WHILE WE'RE YOUNG

THE FINALISTS 2010
HEROES

IN SUPPORT OF
HELP for HEROES

ONE DIRECTION
ONE WAY OR ANOTHER

RED NOSE DAY

STAR!

WISHING ON A STAR

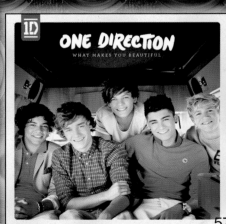

ONE DIRECTION
WHAT MAKES YOU BEAUTIFUL

LOOK TO THE FUTURE

One Direction have already had such an amazing career so far, jam packed with so much success that it's hard to imagine them getting any bigger and better; but who knows what might happen in the not so distant future.

Here are a few predictions!

Love and Marriage?

So, we all know that the boys are still relatively young and won't be settling down just yet. However, 10 years down the line we might have one of the biggest events ever on our hands: a One Direction wedding! Which of the band do you think will be the first to marry and have a family? Harry seems to be the member of the band with an eye for the more mature-minded ladies so maybe it will be him. Only time will tell!

TV Shows?

We know that the boys have already been involved in several TV shows, documentaries, AND their own movie following their lives. So how would you feel about One Direction becoming the next BIG reality TV stars on a regular, full time basis? We think that they could definitely give 'The Kardashians' a run for their money, and what could be better than a tell-all, fly on the wall, reality TV show that followed the boys around everywhere for a year at a time and revealed all of their deepest, darkest secrets?

More Awards

It's a pretty safe bet that 1D will win more awards over the next few years of their career. If they keep releasing great tracks, the fans will keep snapping them up and earning them more prestigious awards from MTV, The BRITS, Nickelodeon and more. What nice additions to their already expanding collection they would be!

Sharing the Wealth

If there is one thing that's for sure, it's that One Direction will always continue to put their fame to good use and for exceptional causes. We're certain that the boys will continue using their popularity to help make a difference to the lives of those who really need it, in any way they can.

Louis has even signed up with Doncaster Rovers in aid of charity, he has been given the No28 squad number for the 2013-14 season and is likely to appear for the team's reserves after signing as a non-contract player. Go Louis!

All The Answers

PICK THE HABIT
page: 21

Worrying — Liam.

Farting — Niall.

Vanity — Zayn.

Falling Asleep — Harry.

Nail Biting — Louis.

QUICK-FIRE LYRICS QUIZ
pages: 26-27

1 Being the way that you are.

2 Just pretending that we're cool.

3 A cup of tea.

4 We take photographs.

5 There's nothing to fix.

WHO'S SHOES
page: 37

A — Harry.

B — Niall.

C — Louis.

D — Zayn.

E — Liam.

KNOW YOUR STUFF - QUIZ
pages: 44-45

1 The X Factor UK.

2 Our Moment.

3 Cry Me a River.

4 Derby County.

5 This is Us!

6 Where we Are.

7 Perrie.

8 At a bakery.

9 Louis.

10 Story.

11 1st February 1994.

12 Kidney – he had one removed as a child

13 Plain White T's 'Hey There Delilah.'

14 White Eskimo.

15 What makes you beautiful.

16 James.

17 Nicole Sherzinger.

18 Isn't she lovely by Stevie Wonder.

19 Up all night.

20 Louis, before joining the band?

WORDSEARCH

p: 36

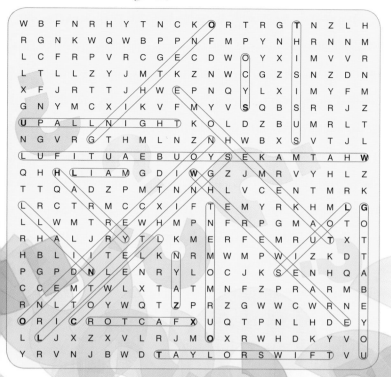

SPOT THE DIFFERENCE

p: 20